THE WATER'S EDGE

EDGE

by

Theresa Rebeck

SAMUEL FRENCH

FOUNDED 1830

New York Hollywood London Toronto

SAMUELFRENCH.COM

IMPORTANT BILLING AND CREDIT REQUIREMENTS

All producers *of THE WATER'S EDGE must* give credit to the Author of the Play in all programs distributed in connection with performances of the Play, and in all instances in which the title of the Play appears for the purposes of advertising, publicizing or otherwise exploiting the Play and /or a production. The name of the Author *must* appear on a separate line on which no other name appears, immediately following the title and *must* appear in size of type not less than fifty percent of the size of the title type.

2ST 2econd Stage Theatre

Carole Rothman *Artistic Director*   Ellen Richard *Interim Executive Director*

presents

THE WATER'S EDGE

BY THERESA REBECK

WITH Kate Burton, Tony Goldwyn, Mamie Gummer, Austin Lysy, Katharine Powell

SET DESIGN BY
Alexander Dodge

COSTUME DESIGN BY
Junghyun Georgia Lee

LIGHT DESIGN BY
Frances Aronson

SOUND DESIGN BY
Vincent Olivieri

ORIGINAL MUSIC BY
Michael Friedman

PRESS
Richard Kornberg & Associates

CASTING
Tara Rubin Casting

PRODUCTION STAGE MANAGER
Roy Harris

STAGE MANAGER
Shanna Spinello

Christopher Burney
Associate Artistic Director

C. Barrack Evans
General Manager

Jeff Wild
Production Manager

DIRECTED BY
WILL FREARS

Second Stage dedicates this production to Wendy Wasserstein, friend of the theatre and champion of women playwrights.

The world premiere of *The Water's Edge* was produced by the Williamstown Theatre Festival

MEDIA SPONSOR
WNYC

CHARACTERS

Helen
Richard
Nate
Lucy

ACT 1
Scene 1

(The back porch of a worn out but still elegant old home, in the country, near a lake. A small pile of junk rests against the baseboard of the porch. Prominent among the junk is an old clawfoot bathtub, covered with a tarp, and an old newel post. There are trees, and a path to a lake. While the place was once elegant, it has fallen in real disrepair. RICHARD stands and stares. Behind him, LUCY.)

RICHARD. The trees. Are like old men. Aren't they? The canopy. Is like a cathedral. I know this place so well. But it's not, it's unlike, like a dream, places you've been that are changed somehow by by the light of your mind, what you know or hope or yearn towards even, rivers running down city streets or or a mansion on a cliff, hovering over a beach you've never seen, the only way to get there is through an endless forest of beech trees... isn't it like that? Is it? I know all of it but I don't know—*(Picking up the newel post, with growing excitement.)* My grandfather. Had a lathe. In the basement. And we would gather, amazed, while he, with his hands, it was a miracle, a piece of wood, so simple, turning, becoming...to be there at the birth of something so beautiful, and not understand, to a child's mind, how it could be, how could it be? I see his hands. It's the same moment. How can it be the same moment?

7

LUCY. Richard...
RICHARD. I'm sorry. But it is the same.
LUCY. There's someone here.

(She looks up at the porch. Someone stands just inside the door, a shadow. RICHARD steps forward.)

RICHARD. Who is it?

(ERICA ENTERS, alert.)

ERICA. Who is it? Excuse me, I think the question is, who are you? I mean, who the fuck are you and you know, what the fuck are you doing here?

(There is a beat. He looks at her.)

ERICA. *(Continuing)* Oh no no. *(Yelling)* Nate! Hey Nate!
RICHARD. Erica.
ERICA. Don't—just—what—Who the fuck is she?
LUCY. I can wait in the car.
RICHARD. No—
ERICA. NATE!
RICHARD. Didn't you know I was coming?
ERICA. I don't even know who you are.

(NATE appears in the doorway. He steps out.)

NATE. What? What? *(Beat)* Wait a minute. Wait—
ERICA. Yes. Yes!
NATE. Dad?

ERICA. Don't call him that!

RICHARD. Erica—

NATE. Oh my god.

RICHARD. Hello.

LUCY. Richard—

RICHARD. No. Stay here. I want you here. This is my friend Lucy.

NATE. Yes, um, really nice to meet you. Does Mom...does she...

RICHARD. I wrote and told her I was coming. Didn't she tell you? I swear. I didn't want to—

ERICA. Fuck you!

RICHARD. Erica—

ERICA. Get out of here!

NATE. Shut up, Erica.

ERICA. No! No! You can't—Nate—

NATE. It's okay!

ERICA. It's not okay! *(To RICHARD.)* You get out of here! Get out of here! Go! Go!

RICHARD. I told her—

ERICA. Fuck you! Just—fuck you, fuck you!

(She goes into the house, slamming the door. There is a tense pause.)

NATE. It's okay. She's just. I mean, it's...well.

RICHARD. I'm sorry.

NATE. No, no, it's good you're here. It's really good.

RICHARD. You're so tall. And handsome. Wow. You're a heartbreaker.

NATE. Yeah. Well. You got, your hair is...different, is it a different color?

RICHARD. I don't think so. I mean, I'm vain, but I'm not foolish. I hope.

NATE. You look different, than I remember.

RICHARD. It's been a long time.

NATE. Yeah. *(Off. ERICA'S EXIT.)* She's, you know—she kind of, just, you can't, because she—

ERICA. *(Inside the house.)* DON'T APOLOGIZE FOR ME!

NATE. I'm not, I'm just saying! *(To RICHARD.)* So, don't, because it's always—and she's great, she's just—you know. *(Beat)* Do you want some tea or something? Iced tea?

(ERICA appears again.)

ERICA. Nate, stop it! You can't—*(To RICHARD.)* I'm sorry. But you can't, I just don't think—

RICHARD. I'd love some tea.

(NATE nods and goes inside. ERICA looks at them. After a moment, she follows NATE inside.)

ERICA. Nate!

(RICHARD and LUCY, alone.)

LUCY. Are you all right?

RICHARD. Fine. I actually, that went better than I thought it would.

LUCY. It did?

RICHARD. *(A wonder.)* He's handsome, isn't he? To see your son, suddenly—it wasn't sudden, okay, but to me—oh my god. Look at this—look at this.

(He pulls the tarp off the bathtub.)

RICHARD. *(Continuing)* My father put this out here when I was a little kid. We would take baths together, under the stars. It was incredible. He hooked the whole thing up to the plumbing in the kitchen, so you could run hot water out here, it was a whole production, and then the two of us would lie back and look up, through the branches, and pick out the stars. Every season. The winter nights. Watching the sky turn. Orion. Cassiopeia.

LUCY. Richard.

RICHARD. You probably can't see anything now, the trees are so overgrown, it's like a medieval forest, almost...

LUCY. RICHARD. *(Beat)* Are you insane? I mean—are you nuts, here? You can't just show up like this. I mean, Jesus! Are you insane? These people don't know you!

RICHARD. These people are my children!

LUCY. Be that as it may. This clearly is not going to turn into A Winter's Tale, with everyone hugging and being so glad. I think we should go.

RICHARD. This is my house. It's my home.

(He settles into the bathtub.)

LUCY. Look. Does your ex-wife know you're coming? I mean, at least she knows you're coming, right?

(NATE comes out again, with iced tea.)

NATE. *(Explaining)* Mom is, somewhere, but I think she said, you know, errands and, so here's the tea. Do you like sugar? Or milk? Sometimes milk, in iced tea, most people don't but it can, or lemon, that's more, but I don't, the milk really seems more soothing. *(A breath.)* Not that we need to be soothed. But not that we don't either, I guess. I think, I could...I think I'll have milk. With the tea.

RICHARD. That sounds great.

NATE. Okay. Here, you can, yourself, I... making tea for other people sometimes seems, I don't know. Too, almost, what we drink, is specific. So.

LUCY. I'll do it.

(She goes and pours tea for herself and RICHARD. NATE shifts on his feet, awkward.)

NATE. I've thought about...well, if you...you know. Ever. Of course I did. It's been a long time.

LUCY. *(Trying to be social.)* How long has it been, exactly?

RICHARD. Seventeen years.

LUCY. Whoa. *(Recovering)* Really. Wow. Oh. That's not—wow. That is a long time. Isn't that funny, I had no idea. I mean, I knew it was—but I—Since you've seen each other? Really?

NATE. It's a long time.

RICHARD. A very long time.

NATE. It's different than I thought it would be. Seeing you. It feels different. I don't know what it feels like.

(He looks at his father, trying to figure out what it feels like.)

RICHARD. I didn't want to stay away. I hope you knew that.

NATE. Oh, I don't—you don't have to say that. It's—

RICHARD. It's true. I asked. So many times. I hope she told you.

NATE. No no, she, uh—no. She didn't.

(RICHARD nods. After a moment, NATE starts to cry.)

RICHARD. Nate.

NATE. Sorry. I'm sorry. Sorry.

(But he continues to cry. RICHARD goes to him, tries to touch him. NATE takes a step backwards, confused. ERICA comes out of the house, quick, and goes to NATE.)

ERICA. Come on. Come on.

(She takes him inside. They are gone. LUCY looks at RICH-ARD.)

LUCY. You're right. This is going so well.

RICHARD. Look. I'm not going to say anything against their mother. But this is not a situation of my making.

LUCY. I'm not criticizing.

RICHARD. You're not?

LUCY. I just, for heaven's sake, Richard, this is—ai yi yi. Seventeen years?

RICHARD. I told you—

LUCY. You said a long time—

RICHARD. Seventeen years is a long time.

LUCY. Seventeen years is a long long time. You haven't seen them ever? During that whole time? Your own children?

RICHARD. It was not a situation of my making!

LUCY. Be that as it may, I should not be here!

RICHARD. I want you here. I can't, anymore, I—Seventeen years. That's not anything I could live with anymore. You understand that, don't you?

LUCY. I do. I do understand that, and I support, you know I—I'm just saying—

RICHARD. *(Upset)* What was I supposed to do?

(Behind them the door opens and shuts. ERICA is there.)

RICHARD. *(Continuing)* Is he all right?

ERICA. Yeah, he's just kind of in shock. That's all. I mean, there's nothing wrong with him. I don't want you thinking he's like screwed up or anything. Because that is so not the case. I mean, he's sensitive, obviously, and this is, you know...it's weird. That's all.

RICHARD. I did write.

ERICA. Yeah, okay. Good. I mean, I didn't understand that, and we're just a little, I mean, I'm sorry about before. Yelling like that. I am really sorry. *(Beat)* You must think we're both freaks.

RICHARD. No.

ERICA. Well, yeah, but how would you know?

RICHARD. I would know.

ERICA. Anyway the point is, this is all a bit unexpected. The house, as you can see, has not even been painted. In years. I keep telling her, but she apparently likes it this way. I don't think it's been painted since you left, in fact. What am I saying I am really just babbling now. What's your name again?

LUCY. Lucy.

ERICA. Do you need to use the bathroom or anything? Did I say that yet? Did Nate offer?

LUCY. No, and I really would just love to maybe wash my face. We've been in that car for what, six hours?

ERICA. Six? Where did you drive from?

RICHARD. We just came up from Philly.

ERICA. Philadelphia? That's where you live?

RICHARD. Yes, why?

ERICA. I don't know, I...Philadelphia. That's...I thought New York, I guess. Didn't you live in New York at some point?

RICHARD. I have a place there too.

ERICA. You have "places" in New York and Philadelphia?

RICHARD. An apartment in New York and a townhouse in Philadelphia, yes. *(Beat)* And, Saint Baart. There's a condo there. *(Beat)* And Telluride.

ERICA. An apartment and a townhouse and a condo and Telluride! And a jet somewhere, probably. I mean, do you have like a yacht and a skimobile and and your own airplane, and—

RICHARD. No. No no, no—*(Beat)* There is a share. In a Lear Jet.

ERICA. So you're, like, a gazillionaire, of course you are.

RICHARD. I sent money. All the time. To you and your brother, and your mother too, I wanted to send, anything you wanted, my hope was, Jesus, I'm sounding pathetic. If there's any way to say this without sounding pathetic, let me just say, I have money. Whatever you want.

ERICA. That doesn't sound pathetic.

RICHARD. Good.

ERICA. No, not good, fuck you, FUCK YOU, it sounds

creepy, you fucking creep! Sorry sorry sorry. I'm sorry. Never mind. This is so fucked. Never mind. I was going to show you to the bathroom, wasn't I? Here, the bathroom is right inside, off the kitchen, here.

(She turns to show her. HELEN stands just inside the doorway. ERICA sees her first.)

ERICA. *(Continuing)* Mom! Hi! You're back from the store, I see. *(Beat)* Look who's here.

(HELEN steps out. She and RICHARD consider each other.)

RICHARD. You got my letter.
HELEN. Yes, I got it. *(To LUCY.)* Hello. I'm Helen.
LUCY. Hi. Lucy. Snow, Lucy Snow.
HELEN. Erica, I think I heard Lucy say she'd like to wash up. Why don't you show her the bathroom?
ERICA. Yeah, I was about to do that.
HELEN. Good.

(ERICA takes LUCY inside. Helen looks at RICHARD.)

RICHARD. Helen.
HELEN. Hello, Richard.

(Pause. They consider each other for a long moment.)

HELEN. *(Continuing)* Men age so well. It really is just enough to make you sick.
RICHARD. *(Taking her in, not condescending.)* You're

still very beautiful, Helen.

HELEN. Oh I have no complaints, I'm perfectly content with my looks. Most women my age are not so lucky. Not that, I don't mean to say women don't age well, that's a terrible thing to say, just awful. We all age. And we're all frightened by it. Women get face lifts. And men get cute little girlfriends. Now, I haven't had a face-life, but apparently you've—how old is she? Don't tell me. The point being that rather puts me one up on you, doesn't it?

RICHARD. Does it?

HELEN. On the fear factor, I think it does.

RICHARD. I think you'll like her.

HELEN. Is that why you brought her? Because you thought we'd like each other?

RICHARD. I wanted you to know each other. I wanted Nate and Erica to meet her.

HELEN. *(Charming)* You haven't seen your children in seventeen years, and you didn't think there would be enough going on to keep everyone entertained without adding a girlfriend into the mix? *(Then)* Sorry. I promised myself I'd be civil. I mean to be civil.

RICHARD. So do I.

HELEN. Good! Let's go back. You look terrific.

RICHARD. So do you.

HELEN. I see Nate served the tea. Iced tea with milk. He started doing it when he was eleven. I'm still not sure why.

RICHARD. It's pretty good.

HELEN. Do you think so? I find it rather disgusting.

RICHARD. Are they living here?

HELEN. Is that a criticism?

RICHARD. Just a question. Most kids, in their twenties,

want to see the world.

HELEN. They have time.

RICHARD. He did all right in college, then?

HELEN. He dropped out after his second year.

RICHARD. And he never went back?

HELEN. It didn't suit him.

RICHARD. So...what does he do with himself?

HELEN. He has a job, in town, at the bookstore. He's been there almost four years now, they love him.

RICHARD. And he's happy with that?

HELEN. He seems to be. Erica finished last spring, up at Brown. History.

RICHARD. History?

HELEN. She has a bent for facts, it seems. She did pretty well. A's and B's, that sort of thing.

RICHARD. And what's she doing now?

HELEN. Living.

RICHARD. Of course.

HELEN. It's not enough for you.

RICHARD. I didn't say that.

HELEN. It's all right. I understand, it must seem odd to someone like you.

RICHARD. You didn't push them, then.

HELEN. Well, Richard, quite frankly, I wanted them here with me. I think I earned that.

RICHARD. Do you think that?

HELEN. You don't get a vote.

RICHARD. You never told them. That I wanted to come back to see them. You never even mentioned—

HELEN. Don't you dare berate me.

RICHARD. I'm here now, Helen. We have to—

HELEN. To what? To be a family again? Is that why you brought your girlfriend?

RICHARD. I want a relationship with my children. You have to make room for that. It's time.

HELEN. Why? Because you say so?

RICHARD. Because it's necessary.

HELEN. I didn't invite you here, Richard. But I don't want to get into some sort of fight about it. I'm willing to be civil.

RICHARD. I'm glad to hear it.

HELEN. If you don't think this is civility, you clearly have forgotten a few things about human behavior.

RICHARD. I haven't forgotten.

HELEN. You've forgotten.

RICHARD. *(Beat)* This is my house.

HELEN. What?

RICHARD. This is my house. I grew up here. It's my home. That's what's been forgotten.

HELEN. *(Beat)* Yes, it has been forgotten, as far as we're concern, that fact has completely evaporated. This is your house? Are you quite sure of that?

RICHARD. I grew up here. I slept in that bedroom, every morning of my life until I was eighteen years old I looked out onto the branches of that tree, every morning, I went fishing in the lake—

HELEN. The lake?

RICHARD. Helen.

HELEN. I can't believe you said that.

RICHARD. I never said you could have it forever.

HELEN. Oh, so forever only applies to certain things and certain people.

RICHARD. Helen.

HELEN. This is not your house.

RICHARD. I left you alone all these years. I gave you the children. I gave you everything you asked.

HELEN. And now what, you want it back? Which, the house or the children?

RICHARD. Helen. What happened is done. We both paid.

(Beat.)

HELEN. No, go on, please. This gets better and better.

RICHARD. It's time. *(Beat)* I'll give you a place to live, that's not a problem, I'm happy to do that. And money, that's not a problem either. But, I do. I want my house back.

HELEN. I confess I am still perplexed by the workings of the male mind. You age well, it's true, but maybe that's because you don't seem to learn anything. Knowledge, life, wisdom, somehow you avoid the whole thing and time just passes you by. I'm not giving you the house back. You can't have the kids, either. You can have your tea. But that's pretty much it.

RICHARD. You said you wanted to be civil.

HELEN. You should talk to Erica about what "civilization" means. It means all sorts of things.

(She heads for the back door.)

RICHARD. I don't want this to go to court. We've kept this out of the courts for so long. You don't want to go there, now.

HELEN. What are you even talking about?

RICHARD. This is not a joke.

HELEN. Am I laughing?

RICHARD. I don't—Helen. I don't want this to be hard.

The last thing I want is to cause more pain, I'm trying not to live in pain anymore. I believe in atonement, I do, but I also believe it's possible to finally rest. To accept the solace of the earth. Being here, finally, I do feel that—that it is perhaps possible. In the air and the wind, the sound of the leaves moving in the dusk, that's not, I can't help but find something, in that, not God, I'm not talking about God or peace or meaning, not that. But something something vivid and whole, sustaining. Larger than all of it. Larger than history. Larger than us.

(A beat.)

    HELEN. It's hard to look at you.
    RICHARD. I know.
    HELEN. *(Shaking her head, sad.)* You want the house back.
    RICHARD. We can talk about it later.

(There is a long moment of silence.)

    HELEN. And now you want to come inside.
    RICHARD. I would like to be asked.
    HELEN. Oh, Richard. You already want too much. You always do.

(She turns and goes to the door. After a moment, she turns, looks at him, and holds open the door.)

    HELEN. *(Continuing)* Please.

(He slowly walks up the steps. Blackout.)

Scene 2

(ERICA, NATE and HELEN. HELEN is shelling peas. NATE is looking at a fancy camera and reading the instruction manual. A beat.)

ERICA. Why are you shelling peas? It's only nine in the morning.

HELEN. I thought I'd make a salad for lunch.

ERICA. Lunch is four hours away.

HELEN. Sometimes I like to be prepared.

(Beat.)

ERICA. Are we going to have to eat with them again? Because, to be frank, dinner last night was not exactly the most fun thing I've ever done in my life.

NATE. I'm glad he came. Sort of. But maybe that was enough. Maybe he should just go now. I mean, are you, do you—

ERICA. Glad? No. Glad is not actually the word I would have used. But I find it interesting that he came and I'm willing to be interested in this situation.

HELEN. Knock yourself out there, Erica.

ERICA. I'm just saying, you know, he wants the house back. I mean, how fucked up is that.

HELEN. How did you hear about that?

ERICA. Well, Mom. Listening at doors?

HELEN. He's not getting the house back.

(ERICA looks over her shoulder, making sure RICHARD isn't around to hear her.)

ERICA. Mom, due respect. Did you ever get him to sign over the deed? I mean, did you? Is it in a document anywhere? In the divorce papers? Because you know, he could kick us out.

HELEN. He's not going to do that.

ERICA. You haven't seen him in seventeen years, how do you know what he's going to do?

HELEN. I just think it's better to be hopeful.

NATE. You—you do?

HELEN. Yes, I do.

ERICA. Well, I think this is war.

NATE. He's—it's not war. I mean—I—how is this war?

ERICA. He showed up with his girlfriend. How imperialistic can you get?

NATE. How is having a girlfriend imperialistic?

ERICA. It's the whole presumption of ownership.

HELEN. Erica, you need to calm down.

ERICA. Oh I do, do I? I mean, look at him. Nice camera, Nate.

NATE. What?

ERICA. Are you just going to let him buy you like that?

NATE. He's not buying me! I'm just—I—it looked kind of, I mean, I never, there are books, in the store about these things and I never, because...

ERICA. Beware of Greeks bearing gifts.

NATE. I didn't see you giving those earrings back.

ERICA. You don't see me wearing them. Gold fucking earrings. Give me a break.

NATE. Yeah, that sucks, somebody gave you gold earrings, your life really sucks.

ERICA. What sucks is he came here to take the house back! And you're just, you're both just—

HELEN. We're not doing anything, Erica.

ERICA. That's my point! The guy's got like six hundred houses all over the planet, and he's showing up here to kick us out. Six hundred houses, not enough, he wants this house, too! And you're just sitting there! Hellooooo—

NATE. He won't kick us out. I mean, he just wouldn't.

ERICA. He wants to, Nate! I heard him.

HELEN. It's not you who would lose the house. I'm sure if you wanted to stay here, were he to move back, he would be happy to have you.

(Beat.)

ERICA. You didn't get the deed, did you?

HELEN. There were some details that were overlooked, over the years.

ERICA. The deed to the house is not a detail, Mom! What kind of a stupid divorce lawyer did you have, anyway?

HELEN. Well, sweetie—technically—there wasn't technically a divorce.

NATE. What?

ERICA. Wait a minute. You're not divorced?

HELEN. I'm afraid there was too much acrimony to pull off an actual divorce.

NATE. You're still married to him? You never told us that.

HELEN. It didn't seem relevant. Besides, you never

asked.

NATE. Why would we ask?

ERICA. No no. That's okay. That's good, that's very good. So you divorce him now, and you say, I have to have the house. He abandoned us for seventeen years, no judge on the planet is going to give him the house after that.

HELEN. Every month, I got a check. He supported us the whole time.

ERICA. So? He should support us.

HELEN. You're still young, Erica. You believe in clarity. Which is fine, but not necessarily useful, in every situation.

ERICA. What does that mean? You keep saying all this stuff, I have no idea what you even mean! There's like no facts, here, Mom! Could you hand over a couple facts once in a while?

HELEN. The facts aren't necessarily relevant.

ERICA. I am going to scream.

HELEN. Please don't.

ERICA. Why are you being like this? Why aren't you mad?

HELEN. It's not that I'm not angry. It's maybe that I'm angry enough not to get too worked up about it.

ERICA. That makes no sense at all.

NATE. I think it does.

ERICA. Jesus Christ, Nate. Would you stop being such a patsy?

NATE. I'm not a patsy. You're—hysterical.

ERICA. This whole family is insane. Did he write and tell you he was coming? Did he? Did he? He wrote and said I'm coming to take back the house? Huh?

HELEN. Yes, actually, he did.

ERICA. So why didn't you do anything?

HELEN. What could I do?

ERICA. You didn't even tell us.

HELEN. I was sort of hoping that he'd reconsider.

ERICA. Well, he didn't do that, did he!

HELEN. No. He didn't.

ERICA. *(Angry)* How could you let him come in? How could you sit there and have dinner with him, and, and—what's her name—

NATE. Lucy.

ERICA. I know her name!

HELEN. I don't know, Erica. Maybe it wouldn't be so bad for you to know your father. As long as he's here anyway.

ERICA. Mom! That is so unbelievably lame I don't even— you have to protect yourself! I'm calling a lawyer. And, in addition, we are going to paint this place. It needs a coat of paint!

(She goes inside the house. NATE looks at HELEN, moves closer to her. He puts his arm around her. She reaches out and takes his hand, kisses it, and goes back to shelling peas.)

NATE. So they're still sleeping, huh?

HELEN. Richard is. He was always a night owl. I believe that Lucy is on her way back up from the lake.

(NATE turns to look, then—)

NATE. I think it'll be okay, Mom. He won't make you go. That would be just, you know. It won't happen. It would be too mean.

HELEN. *(Beat)* I'm glad you think the world isn't mean.

NATE. No, I know it's mean. But people aren't. Necessarily. I don't think. It's, you know, everybody thinks they're right, and more like that, is what I think. I don't know what I think. But he can't, I don't think—what he said? Yesterday? He said some things, I think, that, I know this is weird. But I just don't think he'll take the house.

(LUCY wet, in a bathing suit, comes up the path.)

LUCY. Good morning.

NATE. Morning.

LUCY. I just went and took a swim.

HELEN. Yes.

LUCY. Well, I guess that's obvious. Of course that's obvious. Anyway. It's beautiful, the water. The way it moves from warm to cold, it's so mysterious, why does it do that?

HELEN. All lakes do that, I've been told.

LUCY. How far across is it?

HELEN. Three quarters of a mile, straight across. If you swim it lenghth-wise, it comes closer to two. There's only a few who do that regularly. Mr. Samuels down the road, he's eighty-three. He's one of those old people who doesn't have anything better to do than show off.

LUCY. He does up and back? That's four miles.

HELEN. It takes him all day.

LUCY. Still.

HELEN. Like I said, he's a big show-off.

LUCY. Do you ever do it? The...

HELEN. I'm not really much of a swimmer.

LUCY. Nate, you must.

NATE. Uh, no.

HELEN. None of us really. Are swimmers.

NATE. Once in a while.

HELEN. Don't lie. Never.

LUCY. God, I'd be down there all the time.

HELEN. Well. People are different, aren't they?

LUCY. No, no, I mean—I do understand why you might not. Swim. I mean, when I was a kid, my parents would take me out to the country and you know, it was always, get in the lake! But I was convinced, out in the middle? I was convinced there were monsters out there, ready to just drag me down.

HELEN. Yes. I think that's the general feeling here.

LUCY. Or sharks.

NATE. *(Awkward)* Sharks don't swim in fresh water.

LUCY. No, I know, but you think of, you know. What lurks. Sharks. Pirhannas.

HELEN. *(Abrupt)* Do you need another towel? Or coffee?

LUCY. I don't drink coffee.

HELEN. Of course you don't.

LUCY. No, well, I mean, I'm not some weirdo health freak, although swimming at the crack of dawn and no coffee, I guess it could seem like I'm on my way to some holy land where you could just take a whole day to do the whole lake. Like what's his name?

HELEN. *(Tight)* Mr. Samuels?

LUCY. It's wild, if you think about that? That at the end of his life, he wants nothing more than to live in the water, day in day out... It's kind of beautiful. The water. Returning to the womb.

(HELEN stands up, taking a breath.)

NATE. Are you okay, Mom?

HELEN. *(Fighting her anger, and losing.)* I'm just, I'm sorry, are you—I just—I'm find this extremely difficult. What is your point. Could you tell me what your point is?

LUCY. *(Startled)* I don't have a point. I just I think it's kind of beautiful. The water—

HELEN. Look. What happened here is really none of your business. I'm not interested in your youthful wisdom about water and wombs and childish versions of Nirvana.

(There is a silence. LUCY looks back and forth.)

NATE. What happened, with Lea, it's still kind of, even though it was a long time ago. That's true. So it's not like, but it is still. You know?

LUCY. *(Beat)* Lea?

(HELEN turns on her, appalled.)

HELEN. Our daughter. Lea. *(Beat)* He hasn't told you anything, has he?

LUCY. I...

HELEN. Died. In the lake. He skipped that part? Well, isn't that convenient. Just skip right over it. Why not. Why not.

LUCY. I'm so sorry.

NATE. You don't just tell people. I mean, I don't, if a customer, oh by the way, my sister drowned in the lake, that'll be twenty-three fifty.

HELEN. I think this is a little different, Nate.

NATE. I know. I'm not saying—I know!   I'm just, I wouldn't either. If I was him. What's the point?

LUCY. I'm so sorry.

NATE. It was an accident.

HELEN. No. You are not allowed to say that. An accident is you look away for one moment, half a moment, he didn't even know it had happened! How long was she in there?

NATE. I don't—

HELEN. *(To LUCY.)* I was the one who found her. He didn't even know. *(Then)* If you go down, in the morning, the light on the water—it's quite extraordinary, really, everything moves. Because the reflection, on the trees, all those subtle greens, everything seems to be moving but nothing, it's a trick of the light.

NATE. Mom.

HELEN. On this side, not—the reflection of the trees across the lake, they're black, almost, the sun is behind them so the shadow cast across the lake, and then, the lily pads, on the shadow, they pick up the sun, all of them so flat and white, and—it was—because you go down, to look, and and you you you have no, no—

NATE. Mom, please—

HELEN. I'm explaining something—

NATE. I know, I just—

HELEN. To see that, in the water. So sure that it must be impossible. She's with Richard. That's not your child. It's a trick of the light.

(Beat. She shakes her head, drops the peas, and goes down the path, to the lake. After a moment NATE clears his throat, speaks.)

NATE. It was pretty bad. That's why he didn't tell you.

LUCY. Is it?

NATE. I mean, I can't even—it was really bad. She kind of lost her mind, that's pretty much all I remember. I mean, I remember some of it, after, I can't remember the specific, how he left, because he, well. It kind of all goes white. When you look back and try to remember it. It's very white, in your head. There's stuff before and stuff after. But right around when it happened? It's all pretty white. *(Off HELEN'S EXIT.)* I wish I could make her brain go white. I think it would be better for her.

LUCY. *(Chagrined)* I am the stupidest woman alive.

NATE. No, no. I mean, he didn't tell you. You didn't know.

LUCY. *(Upset)* I went for a swim! I mean how—oh, god—that's just—oh, Jesus—

NATE. A lot of people swim in the lake.

LUCY. Yes, yes, I'm sure, but this is a little different! I mean, you know, I—oh, god. This is just—you know, oh, he just forgot to mention—

NATE. It's really hard to talk about. I mean, she acts like oh he should have told you, but we don't talk about it. We don't talk about anything! Get this. She just told us not ten minutes ago, they aren't even divorced. I mean, for how long, seventeen years, my own parents! And I didn't even know!

LUCY. They're not divorced?

NATE. No. But the thing is, I don't really think it's deliberate. Some things are just hard to talk about. You know, I mean, I'm trying not to sound, about, because it was awful, like I said, but it was seventeen years ago. You know, seriously—seriously, it was terrible, but what can you do about it now?

(A beat. LUCY looks at him.)

LUCY. So why talk about it.

NATE. That's right.

LUCY. So that's why he didn't say anything.

NATE. Well, yeah, I mean, especially since...never mind.

LUCY. *(A beat.)* There's more?

NATE. No! Not really. I mean—no. He just...I mean. *(Beat. She looks at him.)* He was kind of, there was some, at least she thinks—he may have been, meeting someone. Else.

LUCY. A woman? He was meeting another woman, when—

NATE. It's hard to say, for sure. I mean, he did—he had done, I mean.

LUCY. Had done what?

NATE. Other, um, women. That's what she says. But, you know. It was a long time ago. *(Beat)* Really. It was such a long time ago.

(They sit in silence, for a moment.)

LUCY. I fall for guys way too fast. It's like a disease, it just is. My therapist just about threw a fit when I told her I had hooked up with Richard, I was supposed to take a year off from men, ha ha. I mean, I totally get why I do it, I had a hideous father, really just nuts, and now I spend way too much time looking for approval from men, any one of them will do. If they're twenty years older and want to boss me around, so much the better.

NATE. I'm sorry.

LUCY. Please don't apologize. I mean, this is, the only thing that could make this situation any worse would be if people started apologizing to me. Because I'm the one, I just, what am I doing here?

NATE. You didn't know.

LUCY. I knew something! I knew something was up! You get that feeling, you know? That feeling? What good is it, having it, if you don't...whatever.

NATE. How did you meet him, anyway?

LUCY. Oh, waiting tables. He sat at one of my tables and flirted with me. Therapy is wasted on me, it just is.

NATE. You're a waitress?

LUCY. No, I'm a highly educated person who is temporarily between things. And then Richard...I mean, I'm not just attaching myself to men. I've studied. I studied journalism, for a while, that just depressed the hell out of me. Everybody was so mean, I just couldn't figure out—I said to this one professor, he was like this major genius, and he was just a motherfucker, and I finally said, why do you think the truth is just the meanest thing you can think of to say? And he told me I was naive and then he said a bunch of other shitty things, I was actually sleeping with the guy, so he felt he had license, I guess. Anyway, that was it for me and journalism. So that's not, that wasn't a good choice, obviously, something else will show up and until then...I'm. sorry. I'm really sorry.

(Beat.)

NATE. I think you're right. About people being mean. I don't believe in that either.

LUCY. No no, well, please, I'm ridiculous, really. I can't believe I even say things like that.
(She holds her head in her hands. NATE goes to her, touches

her arm. She looks at him. RICHARD appears in the door-
way checking his cell phone.)

RICHARD. Fuck. Can't you get a fucking sugnal out here?
Lucy, you take a swim? Isn't the lake incredible?

(LUCY moves away from NATE.)

RICHARD. *(Continuing)* What a morning. It's amazing,
being here, after all this time, you'll have to forgive me for
turning into a babbling lunatic for a day or two, but it's truly so
overwhelming just to be here. I forgot—or I didn't forget, I just
didn't let myself fully remember. How much a place, a specific
place—this place—can fill you or... forget it. I am babbling. Oh
hey, Nate, you try this thing out yet?

(He picks up the camera, starts to fiddle with it.)

RICHARD. *(Continuing)* I got one of these for myself last
year; the technology is amazing. They can do everything except
cook dinner for you. Except yours is a newer model, so maybe
it can do even that now. Here, let me show you...
LUCY. Richard. You have told me nothing. You piece of
shit.

(There is a moment, then—)

NATE. I'm going to go see how Mom is.

(He heads down the path, to the lake.)
RICHARD. What... okay. What...

LUCY. *(Angry)* You brought me here. You told me nothing. You knew I would find out, how could I not find out, in the most humiliating way possible.

RICHARD. *(Beat)* They told you about Lea.

LUCY. You think?

RICHARD. I was going to tell you.

LUCY. Oh when? Around the time you filled me in on how you're still married to another woman—

RICHARD. You wouldn't have come.

LUCY. No, I would not have come! You, that was why it all, yes? Why they made you leave? Because you let your own child drown in this lake that you now think is so fucking BEAUTIFUL—

RICHARD. We both lost our daughter! And then I lost everything else. She, couldn't, and so I—she insisted I go—no visitation, nothing, just—I sent them money, all these years, I paid for anything they, and I didn't ask for anything. There was no way back in but just to come. You see that. You must see that.

LUCY. You were meeting another woman.

RICHARD. *(A beat, then.)* That's between me and Helen.

LUCY. Oh, fuck you.

RICHARD. You think there's a reason! There's no reason! When children die, there is no reason! She needs my guilt. And I gave it to her. I let her have it so that she had a story, everybody, we all have to think something, there has to be a story, doesn't there, otherwise it's too—*(Beat)* There is no story. And I don't want this to sound cold, but I have moved on. I lived in grief for a long time, and I'm not living there anymore. And I wanted you here. I'm not apologizing for that, either. I need a witness. That I am living in the present. While I face all of it.

LUCY. *(A beat, then very plain.)* This idea, this whole, coming here, this is a disaster, Richard.

RICHARD. I don't believe that. This is my home. This is where I belong.

(He goes into the house. LUCY stands, still. Blackout.)

Scene 3

(Late afternoon. NATE is moving a small table out from the side of the house, while HELEN counts and cleans silverware in a basket.)

NATE. I'm not sure the legs still work. They're pretty rusted.

HELEN. I tried one of them this morning. It seemed all right.

(NATE starts to set up the legs.)

HELEN. *(Continuing)* This will be nice, having dinner out here. We used to do it, when you were little, we'd set up that very table and have a party, don't you remember?

NATE. No.

HELEN. It wasn't that often. Your father always enjoyed it more than I did. I found it buggy. But tonight there's a breeze, it should be fine.

NATE. Is Lucy coming?

HELEN. I don't know.

NATE. I can't figure out why she's with him.

HELEN. He's handsome. Like you.

NATE. So?

HELEN. Well, that's not everything, but it's not nothing.

NATE. You think he's handsome?

HELEN. Not as handsome as you, but handsome. Is he still down there? With Erica?

NATE. I think so.

HELEN. I can't imagine what they have to talk about, for all this time.

NATE. Yeah but you told her. You said—maybe she should get to know him. Since he's here anyway.

HELEN. I know what I said, Nate, you don't have to repeat it back to me. I'm just saying. Down at the lake? You'd think he'd have the decency, if he wanted to take a walk with his daughter—the one that's actually alive, I mean—to take a stroll into town. But he was never the most sensitive of men, even given all that poetry he takes to spouting. Does he actually think we buy that, do you think? I'm not criticizing. What would be the point? It's not like he's staying. But it does make you wonder. If he buys it himself. Given reality, such as it is. Back in town for a couple days, just thought I'd drop by, maybe I'll take my daughter for a walk around the lake.

NATE. They're probably on their way back right now.

HELEN. And what about her? This girlfriend? Let's take a lovely swim.

NATE. It wasn't her fault, Mom.

HELEN. *(Snapping)* Don't tell me whose fault it was!

(She looses control of the silverware, which goes flying. She looks at it. NATE starts over, to help clean it.)

HELEN. *(Continuing)* I'm sorry. Leave it, Nate, would you

leave it? You're not my slave for god's sake.

NATE. I know, I—

HELEN. I'm upset. *(Beat)* Him showing up. I'm not going to lie, why should I? Even the sight of him. The comfort of thinking him dead. Always ruined once a month, he had to keep sending those checks, his gesture of remorse, money, every month here comes the money, I'm still out here, look how successful I am. That's not enough. Now he has to show up, in the flesh. Here I am. The flesh of me is still in the world. Flesh and money. LEAVE IT NATE.

(For NATE has reached over, and is trying to clean up the silverware.)

HELEN. *(Continuing)* I'm not incapable! I can do this!

NATE. I know you can—

HELEN. No matter how much has been asked of me, I can do it! That is the one thing I think I can say. After all this time. After everything? I do what is asked of me.

NATE. Why don't you tell him to go?

HELEN. *(Beat)* I know, I know. It's what I should do.

NATE. He doesn't need the house—

HELEN. That's not why he's here.

NATE. It's not?

HELEN. You're so naive. I love you so much, sweetheart, but you are NAIVE.

(NATE flinches. HELEN, trying to calm herself, doesn't notice.)

HELEN. *(Continuing)* Every gesture is a—I want the

house. Here's my girlfriend! I want my kids. What else do you think he wants?

NATE. I don't know. I just think you should tell him, you should tell him—

HELEN. *(Flaring again.)* I don't have to tell him anything! This isn't a conversation! He's not "talking" about anything. He's just taking. You think I don't know him by now? I had three children with that man. And now he's here again, and even after all this time, after all this time, do you think I don't know who he is, and what he wants?

NATE. I don't know, Mom. I don't—I don't—

(LUCY comes out on the porch.)

LUCY. Hi.

NATE. *(Upset)* Hi.

LUCY. We're having dinner out here. How lovely.

HELEN. *(Cool)* It was Richard's idea. Nate was just getting the candles. And the napkins. Don't forget the napkins, sweetie, you always forget.

(NATE goes. LUCY comes down the steps, cautious.)

LUCY. Is there anything I can do?

HELEN. No. Thank you.

(HELEN opens a tablecloth which is on the stairs, brushes the leaves off of it, and drapes it over the card table, as LUCY continues to speak.)

LUCY. I'm sorry.

HELEN. Excuse me?

LUCY. I just wanted to say I'm sorry. For...well... I mean I think it's obvious I'm a little out of the loop here.

HELEN. Yes, well. He's here now, that part is done. The rest, we'll just have to get through.

LUCY. Well. I know that's what he wants. He's been talking for so long about coming. As long as I've known him. So I thought it would be a kindness, to help him get here.

HELEN. A kindness.

LUCY. Yes. I mean, I didn't know about—so now, it seems—

HELEN. Yes.

LUCY. I just wish I had known more. But he really, when he spoke to me, about what this might mean to him—he's very eloquent. So I told him he should come. I thought I was helping, now I'm not so...I don't know. You want me to, maybe if I could help set the table or something...

HELEN. No no, I have it. There is something, though. If you want to help. That you could do for me. For all of us.

LUCY. Sure, anything.

HELEN. If we could have the evening.

LUCY. Have the evening?

HELEN. Richard and I. And the children.

LUCY. Oh.

HELEN. I hope you don't mind.

LUCY. You want me to leave.

HELEN. Just for tonight.

LUCY. Uh. Well.

HELEN. I know why you're here.

LUCY. *(Surprised, unsure.)* You do?

HELEN. And I appreciate, why you're here. I do, I appreciate that.

LUCY. Well, I, I, I—

HELEN. It just might give us a little room. To understand each other. There are a couple terrific restaurants over in Neponset. And the drive is beautiful, especially this time of year.

LUCY. Okay. I see. Sure. *(Beat)* You don't mind, do you mind if I talk to Richard about this?

HELEN. I don't know what your relationship with Richard is like. Is that how you work things out?

LUCY. No. I mean—

HELEN. You do whatever you need. I just ask you, as a favor.

(NATE comes out with napkins, candles and glasses. His arms are much too full.)

NATE. I couldn't, there weren't enough in the kitchen so I had to go to the closet, upstairs. Are these the ones you meant?

HELEN. They're fine. But we'll need the good wine glasses. I'll get them.

(She heads up the steps.)

NATE. It's such a little table. I guess we should just put people around. Like on corners.

HELEN. No no, sweetie. Lucy's not staying. Only four places.

(She goes inside before LUCY can say anything. NATE looks at her.)

NATE. You're not going to be here.

LUCY. Yeah, I might not be here, I guess.

NATE. Where are you going?

LUCY. I guess I might go to Neponset, for dinner. And the drive.

(He starts to set the table. LUCY sits, thinking about this. Suddenly NATE sits down, frustrated.)

NATE. Oh great. I mean, that is just—you're just going to leave? You're kidding! So we're, what, we're expected to have some sort of family dinner? Why?

LUCY. I don't know. I—

NATE. *(Upset)* Why does she want this? Why? Why do we have to do this? Why?

LUCY. I think she—

NATE. You don't know! How could, because why? I don't want it! I thought I did, but you know, I just, everything was fine! It was fine. I want to go back. This is just, there's nothing that can, we need to go back, just back, you know. Back. Not back. Not all the way back, that's not, oh, god, you know, I just—I'm just insane. Obviously. I'm sorry.

LUCY. You're not insane.

NATE. No, of course not. I don't really think that. But like, dinner! I mean. Dinner.

(LUCY doesn't know what to say. ERICA and RICHARD arrive, coming up from the lake. RICHARD is enthusiastic.)

RICHARD. The beauty of this place is really such a tonic! The trees, the air, it's like wine, you can get drunk on it!
(LUCY takes a step back from NATE, who quickly turns away.

Somehow, LUCY manages to look a little guilty.)

RICHARD. *(Continuing)* Everything okay?
LUCY. Sure.
RICHARD. Nate?
NATE. Yeah. We're just getting ready for dinner. I'll go help Mom.

(He hurries into the house. RICHARD looks at LUCY.)

RICHARD. What's that about?
LUCY. Nothing.
ERICA. Well, maybe I'll see if I can help with dinner, too.

(She heads after him.)

RICHARD. No, no stay! Erica and I were just walking down to the pier, to see my old dingy, it's still there, if you can believe that.
ERICA. *(Cool)* Yep. Pretty amazing.
RICHARD. You mentioned you had some plans to paint the house!

(He gestures to the house, trying to keep her in conversation. She is barely civil.)

ERICA. It's not actually plans.
RICHARD. Okay, so what are you thoughts?
ERICA. My "thoughts" are, the house could use a coat of paint.
RICHARD. You thinking about changing the color?

ERICA. I'm not thinking about anything other than it needs a coat of paint!

RICHARD. Well, I'm not going to argue with you about that. This place could use a little TLC.

ERICA. What did you say? "TLC?" Did you actually say that?

RICHARD. You just said yourself, it needs a coat of paint. That's the least of it. The porch is rotted through, we'll have to look at that first, no point in painting wood that's rotten.

ERICA. You're not painting anything. What are you even talking about?

RICHARD. *(A beat.)* I just mean, if it's something you want to tackle, I'll help. You're not the only one who loves this house.

ERICA. That doesn't give you rights. You left. You were not here. Love doesn't give you rights!

RICHARD. Are you sure about that?

ERICA. Yes, as a matter of fact, I am. I am quite sure about that.

(She heads into the house.)

RICHARD. Do not just walk away from me. Please. I want to talk about this; that's why I'm here. I'm your father.

ERICA. *(Turning, pissed, taking up the gauntlet.)* **Okay** then. *(To LUCY.)* Due respect to you, which I know this is none of your business—*(To RICHARD.)* But like, are you going to take the house? Is that really your plan here?

RICHARD. Your mother and I—

ERICA. Don't change the subject. You just said right now, right here in front of witnesses, that you want to talk to me, you're my dad, love gives you rights, blah blah blah, well, the elephant in the room, "Dad," is the house and what you think you mean when you say you want it back. Because you know, okay, I'll tell you, you want to know me, I'll tell you what I did today, I called a lawyer to find out what kind of rights you do have in this situation, and the fact is, you have quite a few. Quite a few, and we have none. So I want to know what you're going to do about that. Because it's kind of hard to "get to know you," "Dad," when we all have a gun to our heads.

(She looks at him. RICHARD looks at her, then finally speaks, simple.)

RICHARD. I don't have a gun to your head, and you don't hate me, even though you want to. This isn't about tearing things down. Enough of that has happened, through nobody's fault.

ERICA. But you still want the house.

(RICHARD looks around.)

ERICA. *(Continuing)* Cut it out and just admit it! You want the house! So I want to know what does that mean, are you going to kick us out? Is that what it means? The irony being of course that you have six thousand other places you could live, what the FUCK do you need our house for?

RICHARD. If I offered you one of the six thousand other houses, free and clear, would you take it?

ERICA. Why should I? This is my house!

RICHARD. Ah, then I'm not the only one capable of being irrational about this place. Thanks, I was just checking.

ERICA. Yeah, that's hilarious. So you honestly expect to

just come back here, and and make us LEAVE—

RICHARD. Cut it out, you know that's not what's going on. Why would I ask you leave? I've spent the last seventeen years wishing I was with you. Why would I ask you to leave, now that I've finally worked up the nerve to come home?

ERICA. This is highly unsatisfying. You're contradicting yourself all over the place.

RICHARD. So are you.

ERICA. I'm not. I'm being very straightforward.

RICHARD. It may be straightforward, what you're saying, but it's not the truth.

ERICA. You don't know me.

RICHARD. Fine. I don't know you. I'm a total stranger. Get your lawyer. Get, whoever you want, to come out here and tell me to leave. Do it.

ERICA. Why, you know—you, you could have, almost any time up to this point! Who are you supposed to be, now? Some creepy rich guy who's going to hang around and just give everybody things, have a camera, hey, let's forget everything that ever happened here, how about some gold earrings?

RICHARD. I just wanted to bring something! All those birthdays and Christmases, all those years I never got to give you anything—

ERICA. And whose fault was that?

RICHARD. It's no one's fault!

ERICA. That's a very convenient position.

RICHARD. Can we stay on the subject?

ERICA. I think we are right on subject. This is exactly—

RICHARD. We were talking about whether on not I am trying to buy your affections with a pair of earrings.

ERICA. It's the same point! The same point! You have not

been here, and you don't know me! Do I look like the kind of person who would give a shit about a pair of earrings? Do I?

LUCY. Richard. Maybe I should—

RICHARD. She wouldn't send me any pictures of you. So I had to imagine everything. And you were so—sweet when you were seven. You liked all that make up, and pink clothes, you always wanted to wear pink. So I thought...just something pretty...

ERICA. I never wore pink.

RICHARD. You wore pink all the time. I have a little shirt, I...

ERICA. You have one of my shirts from when I was seven?

(Beat.)

RICHARD. I just wanted to bring something. A pair of earrings, seemed...I'm sorry if it was foolish. You don't like earrings, you're right, I didn't know. I don't know you. *(Beat)* You can exchange them.

ERICA. That's not the point! Oh, never mind. This is a nightmare.

RICHARD. Tell me how to help. Tell me what I could do, to make this easier. *(Beat)* Do you want me to leave?

(ERICA looks at him, looks away. For a long moment, she tries to think of something to say.)

ERICA. You—that was your boat? I mean, that boat down there? Was really your boat?

RICHARD. My father gave it to me. When I was twelve.

We'd take it down to the far end of the lake, where the catfish run.

ERICA. Did you ever catch any?

RICHARD. Catfish? *(Beat)* Yeah. Trout, too. Once, not a lot, just once.

(There is another moment of silence. ERICA sighs, finally.)

ERICA. I've never been fishing in the lake. It's sort of the unspoken rule here. No one goes on the lake.

RICHARD. I'll take you fishing.

ERICA. Are you kidding? Oh please. That would be, I don't...

RICHARD. Times change. I'll take you fishing.

(She looks at him, not trusting this, more and more upset.)

ERICA. I'm sorry. I can't do this. I can't, I just, I'm really, I'm sorry—

(He goes to her, concerned now.)

RICHARD. Erica, please. It doesn't have to be this hard. It doesn't.

(He touches her arm. She suddenly hugs him. He holds her for a moment. Behind them, HELEN watches from the door-way.)

HELEN. Everything okay?
(ERICA pulls away, sudden.)

ERICA. Sorry. I was just coming in. To help with dinner.

(She shakes her head at the lameness of this, then goes inside, leaving LUCY and RICHARD and HELEN.)

HELEN. Lucy, maybe you could give me a hand with these.

LUCY. Sure.

(HELEN hands her glasses, and they continue to set the table in silence for a moment.)

LUCY. *(Continuing)* Richard, um...I have to...uh, Helen has mentioned that maybe I might want to, I guess, take off for the evening. She seems to think it might be a good idea for me to have dinner in someplace called Neponset.

RICHARD. Helen asked you to go...somewhere else to dinner?

LUCY. Yes.

RICHARD. Why?

HELEN. I thought she might like to see it, as long as she's up here. You remember, it's a terrific little town, and the drive is sensational. You just take a left, out of the drive, and then right when you get to route twelve. It's a straight shot from there. The trees are magnificent.

RICHARD. I'm sorry, I'm just—catching up here. Run this by me again. You asked my girlfriend to leave?

(It's a direct challenge. HELEN sighs and looks at him.)

HELEN. Actually, Richard, I didn't ask her to leave. I

asked you to leave.

RICHARD. Yeah, okay—

HELEN. You were the one who came without invitation. I was just making an attempt to be a good sport about it.

RICHARD. So asking Lucy to leave is being a good sport.

HELEN. Since—you are not leaving—and since you claim you're here to get to know your children—in addition to taking our house from us—

RICHARD. This is classic.

HELEN. How so, Richard? Since that is what you claim to be here for, and since I apparently have very little choice in the matter, I thought I would make an attempt to actually help you out. She can stay. I told her, it was up to her. If it makes you both uncomfortable, we'll just set an extra place. It's not a big deal. You've both already made much too much of it.

(She goes back to the table. RICHARD watches her, eyes narrowed.)

LUCY. Well, that's good. I mean, thank you, Helen, because I was feeling, a bit—

HELEN. I didn't mean for it to cause even a moment's insecurity on anyone's part. I'm sorry it did.

LUCY. No, it's not that—

HELEN. Say no more about it. It's done! Let me just get an extra place setting.

(She heads for the house.)

RICHARD. *(Sudden)* No. No, it's fine. I'm sorry. It's fine, Lucy. Helen's right. I need to spend some time with the kids.

LUCY. Richard, for heaven's sake—

RICHARD. You've been such a trooper, you should take the night off.

LUCY. Richard, could you and I please, just can we have a momement of privacy to discuss this?

HELEN. Of course.

RICHARD. No, it's fine, Helen. We don't have to talk about it. It's already way too big a deal.

(Beat.)

HELEN. So...we're okay about this?

RICHARD. We're fine.

HELEN. Good. Oh good, the brussel sprouts. Nate, did you remember the mint jelly?

(RICHARD hands LUCY his car keys. ERICA comes out, carrying a bowl of vegetables. NATE, behind her, carries a lamb roast.)

NATE. Yes, you told me eight times.

HELEN. Well, sometimes you're a little lightheaded, sweetheart.

(NATE turns and looks at LUCY.)

NATE. Are you going?

HELEN. Who's got the wine?

ERICA. I'll get it.

(She goes.)

HELEN. *(Before LUCY can answer.)* What about the orzo?
Nate!

NATE. Okay!

(He turns to go inside.)

LUCY. Richard—

RICHARD. Goodbye, Lucy.

ERICA. *(Coming out, with wine.)* Does anyone want
white?

HELEN. It's a lamb roast, sweetie.

ERICA. I know the red meat rule, Mom. But some people
like white anyway.

RICHARD. Red's great.

LUCY. *(A beat, then.)* Yeah. Okay. Goodbye.

(She starts to go.)

RICHARD. This looks sensational. Here, let me help you
with that.

HELEN. Thank you.

*(He moves a chair for HELEN, whose hands are full. After a
    moment, LUCY goes around the side of the house, leaving
    while the others sit down to dinner. Blackout.)*

END ACT ONE

ACT II

Scene 4

(An hour later. NATE, ERICA, HELEN and RICHARD are under the stars, eating dinner. RICHARD looks up at the sky.)

RICHARD. Cassiopeia. Orion's belt, is that Orion?

HELEN. It's amazing you can pick that out, the trees block most of it.

RICHARD. The trees weren't so full forty years ago. I can still see the sky, plain, in full view. It's there, and not there. Memory. You know what we should do? We should take the boat out. My brother and I used to do that. Middle of the night, from the center of the lake, the night sky is beyond imagining.

ERICA. Maybe we could fish.

NATE. Now?

ERICA. It's night. That's when fish come out.

NATE. Fish sleep. I mean, don't they? Sleep? Because— never mind.

RICHARD. No, she's right, right at dusk, as the stars are

coming out, that's when they feed. We could do it. I went down to the basement and took a look at the tackle just before, it's in pretty good shape, all things considered.

HELEN. You went downstairs and checked the fishing tackle? Why did you do that?

RICHARD. I mean—I'm sorry. It's not such a good idea. We'll try it another night.

ERICA. Is there going to be another night?

RICHARD. Of course there is.

(There is a pause. HELEN pours wine.)

RICHARD. *(Continuing)* Thank you. *(Beat)* So, Nate. You're working in a bookstore. How is that?

NATE. How is it?

RICHARD. Do you enjoy it?

NATE. Yes.

RICHARD. What do you do down there?

NATE. You know, you—help people find the books they want to buy and then you go to the cash register and you ring it up, and then you take their credit card and run it through the slot, and wait for the approval, and then you get them to sign the slip, and then you put their books in a bag, most people actually don't want a bag, up here people are environmentally conscious, but sometimes you give a bag and a little bookmark that has the logo of the store, and then it's like that.

RICHARD. Sounds terrific.

NATE. I also unpack the books out of the boxes, and figure out where to put them on the shelves. Sometimes that's not, like, easy, because you have something like you know, Primo Levi, Survival at Auschwitz? Where do you put that, under biography or history? You have to make a decision, about stuff like that.

RICHARD. So there is some challenge to it, that's good.

NATE. Well, that's—I don't, you know, I, it's not brain surgery or anything, obviously—

RICHARD. No, no, I—I just meant—

NATE. I don't think it's—because people come in, some new people, all the time, or there are a lot of people in the, around the, who read a lot, and want to know, mysteries are, when they come in, there's always a few people waiting and you talk to them and, or there's one guy who used to teach, not at a big college or anything, but he still, it's like he's, last week he came in and he was looking for War and Peace, because he never—and I, because he read Moby Dick, which he also never, and he thought—you know, how did he ever get to this place. Where he's like seventy or something. Without reading War and Peace. So we talked about that, and I found it for him. *(Beat)* Sometimes I think, you know, he doesn't have a lot of people to talk to, so when he comes into the book store, that's, you know. Anyway. *(Beat)* I need to get some water.

(He stands up and goes into the house.)

ERICA. *(Defensive)* Look. It's not like he's a freak or anything.

RICHARD. I know that.

(ERICA stands and goes into the house after him. After a moment, RICHARD looks at HELEN.)

RICHARD. *(Continuing)* All I said was—

HELEN. What you said was, "So there is some challenge to it, that's good."

RICHARD. I didn't say it like that.

HELEN. You didn't have to.

RICHARD. Well, it sounds like he's given up. He's twenty six years old. Why has he given up?

HELEN. Maybe he wants other things out of life.

RICHARD. You won't always be here to take care of him.

HELEN. *(A beat.)* You are really something. You haven't learned anything in seventeen years. Have you? You're exactly the same person. Of course, why wouldn't you be.

(She starts to clear the table.)

RICHARD. That's not exactly helpful.

HELEN. *(Hissing)* Oh, now I'm supposed to be helpful? You want help now? From me? You want me to help you—help you—

RICHARD. Hey. Hey, hey.

(He reaches over and takes her hand.)

RICHARD. *(Continuing)* I'm sorry. I'm sorry this is so hard.

(They look at each other for a moment. RICHARD'S hand stays on hers. She finally moves, goes to finish cleaning the table. He watches her in silence. Finally, NATE comes back out onto the porch, with ERICA.)

NATE. I can—I can do that, mom.

HELEN. *(Subdued)* It's okay, I've got it.

(She picks up some plates and goes into the house.)

NATE, Maybe, I can just start on the dishes with you, that way—

ERICA. Mom can do that, Nate. She's fine.

HELEN. Of course I am.

ERICA. Come on, you're freaking out over nothing. Richard just wants to talk about, like, what we've been doing our whole lives. That's all.

NATE. I'm not freaking out! I was just getting a drink of water!

ERICA. No, I know. But Mom can start on the dishes herself.

(She pushes NATE a little. He goes down the steps. Behind them, HELEN watches for a moment, then goes inside.)

RICHARD. I am interested in what you're doing. *(Beat)* I mean, I love bookstores. Working in a bookstore. That seems to be a very elegant occupation.

NATE. *(Beat)* I like the books.

RICHARD. Do you read a lot?

ERICA. Constantly. You should see his room, there are like piles of books around his bed. He reads like a book a day, it's ridiculous.

RICHARD. A book a day! Come on.

NATE. What?

RICHARD. Well, a book a day, that's—That's impressive. I mean, that's more than impressive, that's—spectacular.

NATE. *(Abashed, but pleased.)* Well, they're not all, some of them are kind of stupid—

RICHARD. They don't all have to be Tolstoy to still be worth reading—

NATE. *(Explaining)* Yeah but some of them are kind of, I mean, like mysteries. Some of them are really dumb. Not dumb, you don't want to judge, I'm not judging, because it's still a book, and books are—

RICHARD. Yes.

NATE. And people! Because people come in, some—they hope, or yearn even, that the person in the bookstore will know, the books will be inside you, and you can tell them, because reading is very, almost to some people, even a dumb mystery is something they hold onto like a chalice, or—I don't know. I'm sorry.

RICHARD. No. No. You're right. Books are holy. I feel that.

NATE. You do?

RICHARD. Yes. Of course. When I'm surrounded by books, it's—

NATE. I know!

RICHARD. I didn't mean, before, that I thought there was something wrong, with working in a bookstore.

NATE. Oh, no.

RICHARD. Because it might have sounded like that. It sounds like something I wish I knew how to do. How to just live so simply, give everything else up, just for the chance to be surrounded by something you think is holy.

NATE. Well. I mean—you're right, I guess I—because that's the best part. I mean, when you're surrounded. By how much love people have in their hearts, when they're looking at books. It's very hopeful. They think, all of them, that the next book they find is just going to be amazing. Even if it's a dumb mystery. And it's so great. Getting to help them find that.

(He smiles at his father.)

RICHARD. What are your favorite ones?
NATE. Oh, I like them all.
RICHARD. All of them?
NATE. *(Excited)* I really do! I like all books. The little kids books, the pictures are so—and the art books and the photography books are always, just—they're easier to just get a sense of than, the history and the biography and the novels of course you have to read the whole thing, or what would be the point? And okay, the literary criticism, or philosophy, that can get a little dense, but—
RICHARD. You read everything?
NATE. What?

(RICHARD is laughing, admiring. He laughs as well, happy.)

RICHARD. And you like them all?
NATE. Well, yeah—
ERICA. Even coffee table books? Like, even books about beading? *(She laughs.)* That was my favorite, one time I stuck my head in his room, he was trying to figure out this workbook about how to make a beaded purse.
NATE. I thought it was interesting!

(They laugh. HELEN steps out onto the porch, carrying a bottle of liquor and two glasses on a tray. She watches this.)

ERICA. Yeah, but that Feng Shui book, Nate. He's in there, reading "Clear Your Clutter with Feng Shui" and he's like surrounded by these piles and piles of books.

NATE. So what's your point?

(They all laugh at this. HELEN watches for a moment before speaking.)

HELEN. Well, this is lovely.

(They look over at her, their laughter fading. She comes down the steps.)

HELEN. *(Continuing)* So what was that all about?

NATE. Nothing.

HELEN. Don't be ridiculous, you were all laughing, what was so funny?

(There is a moment of silence.)

RICHARD. Nate was telling me about his work.

HELEN. And that's funny?

NATE. *(Embarassed)* It wasn't anything. Really. It, I didn't, it wasn't anything.

HELEN. You don't want to tell me?

NATE. It was about, it was stupid. About this book I read on Feng Shui. It was stupid.

(A beat.)

HELEN. Maybe you could start on those dishes, Nate. I'd really appreciate that.

NATE. Yeah, okay.
HELEN. Erica, could you help him?
ERICA. Well—
HELEN. Your father and I have a lot to talk about.
NATE. Yeah, no, of course. Come on, Erica.
ERICA. Okay. Would you not rip my shirt, I said okay!

(She snaps at NATE, as he tugs at her sleeve, but she goes with him.)

RICHARD. *(As she goes.)* Those earrings look beautiful, Erica. They suit you.
ERICA. Thanks. I think they're pretty.

(She goes. After a moment, HELEN hands RICHARD the bottle.)

HELEN. I remember you liked the occasional after dinner drink.
RICHARD. Yeah, thanks. You want some?
HELEN. No.

(He pours.)

RICHARD. You can't just send them off the instant we start getting along. It's not right, Helen.
HELEN. We have things to talk about, Richard. There's no point in putting it off.
RICHARD. I'm not putting it off. I'm just making an observation. You didn't seem too terribly interested in actually talking to me about anything until I started hitting it off with

them. I'm just asking you to consider what that might mean to me, after all this time—

HELEN. Why, because you're so considerate of my feelings, showing up out of nowhere—

RICHARD. I wrote and told you I was coming.

HELEN. With your girlfriend. A particularly considerate touch.

RICHARD. She's not here now. I let you get away with that.

HELEN. You "let me?"

RICHARD. For god's sake, Helen, you were so transparent. Quite frankly, I think you've lost your touch over the years.

HELEN. And yet, I did manage to get rid of her.

RICHARD. Yes you did.

HELEN. My motives being what, might I ask?

RICHARD. Your motives I'm sure will reveal themselves, as they always did.

HELEN. As do yours.

RICHARD. My motives aren't secret. I've told you what I want.

HELEN. Not all of it, Richard. You never show your full hand.

RICHARD. You know what? Maybe you don't know me as well as you think you do. After all this time. I mean, I'm trying, here, and as a matter of fact, I think I'm doing pretty well.

HELEN. Of course you do. After seventeen years, you manage to have a two minute conversation with your grown children, and that means everything's going to work out for you and them, you can just come back and reclaim all of it, and it will all be perfect, is that how it's supposed to be?

RICHARD. I don't know how it's supposed to be. I just know, you can't keep fighting me, because I'm not going away.

HELEN. I'm not fighting! *(Beat)* I don't want to fight. *(Beat, calling.)* Erica, get away from the door!

(ERICA calls from just inside.)

ERICA. Okay, but don't forget to ask about the house!

(HELEN stands and prowls to the edge of the clearing, restless.)

RICHARD. *(Laughing)* She's really something.

HELEN. At least one of them meets with your approval. But you always had a soft spot for her.

RICHARD. They're both wonderful. You've done a wonderful job. *(Beat)* And the meal was terrific.

HELEN. Richard, please stop complimenting me, you sound almost insane, and it's not helping.

RICHARD. I thought you didn't want to fight.

HELEN. This isn't fighting. When we're fighting, you'll know it.

RICHARD. This is just the foreplay, then.

HELEN. What did you say?

RICHARD. Helen, relax, I was kidding. I know it's hard for you. That I'm here. I was just trying to keep things light.

HELEN. Yes, I guess you would prefer that. To keep things light. To act as if that's what our lives were. Full of light.

RICHARD. Who wouldn't prefer that? You should try it sometime.

HELEN. Guess what, we're about to start fighting.

RICHARD. No, we're not. I'm sorry, I'm just, honestly, I know this is hard, impossible, even, but I can't seem to feel anything except happy. Just, really happy to be here. Remember the first time I brought you here? During college, Mom and Dad were gone visiting someone, I don't remember who, and we had the whole place to ourselves. We just made a wreck out of every room, remember? Leaving our clothes everywhere, eating whatever we wanted, making love in the bathtub—

HELEN. Richard.

RICHARD. I can't help it. I don't just remember what went wrong. I remember all of it. How good it was. I should have made you leave with me. It was a mistake, letting you stay here.

HELEN. You "let" me—

RICHARD. It just might have given you some room—

HELEN. Like you?

RICHARD. Yeah, like me. To move on.

HELEN. If you've moved on, then why are you here now?

RICHARD. *(Frustrated)* Look, would you just look around you? It's so beautiful, the trees, the water, the air, it's so—impersonal. Serene. You accuse me of moving on, and I admit it, but so has this place. The trees don't care anymore. The earth—it doesn't care.

HELEN. Well. That's pretty convenient for you, then, isn't it?

RICHARD. Helen, you know, the fact is, you need to let me help you.

HELEN. Help me.

RICHARD. You're just stuck here—

HELEN. Yes, I am, and I didn't ask you to come back and "help" me. You just remember that. I told you to stay away.

RICHARD. That was not going to work forever! It never would, and you knew that, all along! You and I both know, it wasn't that I didn't love you.

HELEN. You know what, Erica's right, we should just talk about the house. If we just keep it on the house, and off the universe—

RICHARD. I don't agree to that.

HELEN. I'm not asking you to agree.

RICHARD. *(Firm, getting to it.)* It was an accident!

HELEN. Don't you fucking tell me it was an accident, there is no such thing as accidents, when my child is dead—

RICHARD. She was my child too—

HELEN. A month. Every summer. I'll clear out, the kids can do what they want, and you can have the house a whole month out of every year. That's what I'll give you. Do you accept my offer?

RICHARD. I want to talk about it. We never talked about it, we just screamed and ripped each other up like animals—

HELEN. Do you accept my offer?

RICHARD. No, I don't!

HELEN. It's all I have to give. If you want more I cannot help you.

RICHARD. It wasn't my fault. It really was just an accident, a terrible, tragic accident, and the way it happened was different, so different than what you—

HELEN. *(Overlap)* Oh, that's what you want. You want history back, you want to change it all, in memory, say it never happened.

RICHARD. I'm not saying it never happened. But what

you thought happened wasn't what happened.

HELEN. It happened as I know it happened and you can't change that now, after all this time you can't suddenly make it all different! You show up saying, nonsense, it's nonsense that you're even here—

RICHARD. It's not.

HELEN. Saying it was different, it was not what I thought, it was only what I thought, every day, it's in my head, you think I don't wish that—you think I didn't want to move on, be impersonal as your fucking trees, you think I don't wish she was never born—but it can't, so don't you—you can't—you—

(She is shaking, inarticulate. He stands, goes to her, and puts his arms around her. She tries to push him away. He won't let her.)

RICHARD. Don't push me away. You need to let me help.
HELEN. There's no help.

(He holds her.)

RICHARD. We should have been able to comfort each other, Helen. It didn't have to end the way it ended.

(She slumps, momentarily, in his embrace.)

HELEN. I wish my brain would be quiet.
RICHARD. I know.

(She lets him hold her for a long moment. Finally, he takes a step back, looks at her, and after a moment, tries to kiss her. She slaps him. He backs away.)

RICHARD. *(Continuing)* I'm sorry. I thought...It's just been so long, that I, away from, you don't want to admit you're just sleepwalking, not living in the center of who you are, we don't get much time here anyway, and struggling, day in and out to live, to just live your life when it's gone, everything, no matter what you do. The loss of everything, it just stood inside me. Like an oak. Time is supposed to move. But it didn't, it just...stopped. *(Beat)* And now to be here. And feel so clear again. So...I...just...

HELEN. It's all right.

(There is a long moment of silence. HELEN wanders the clearing for a moment, looks off at the lake.)

HELEN. *(Continuing)* It does stand inside you. Time. But it's not like a tree. It doesn't grow into anything. It just stands there. Waiting. *(Beat)* It's so strange, to see you, and to not... merely hate you.

RICHARD. That's good.

HELEN. Is it?

RICHARD. Of course it is.

HELEN. I remember that time you brought me here. That first time. How happy we were, just to...we couldn't stop, that whole week, we just...we were so alive. I miss being that person.

RICHARD. You are still that person.

HELEN. I don't know.

RICHARD. You are all of it. Who you were when we met, who you were after it happened. The last time I saw you, you were so—

HELEN. I know what I was.

RICHARD. All of that—and your younger self, too—

HELEN. I can't do this. I have to go in. I have to, Richard, I CANNOT DO THIS.

RICHARD. Helen. Listen. You have to just let me tell you this one thing, please. It will make a difference. It didn't happen, the way you think it did. There was no one else there. I know you thought that. But it wasn't true.

HELEN. You were meeting someone.

RICHARD. I wasn't.

HELEN. That woman. Renting the house at the end of the, she was flirting with you all summer, and I saw her, Richard. I saw her going down there, to the lake, you were meeting—

RICHARD. *(Overlap)* That woman flirted with everyone, I don't even remember her name—

HELEN. She, I saw her going to the lake—

RICHARD. I don't know what you saw, but she wasn't there. I wasn't cheating, Helen.

HELEN. You—

RICHARD. I wasn't cheating. I know you thought that because I had, I don't deny I—But that was over, and you were what I wanted, we were so clear on that, both of us, when—

HELEN. You were, Richard—

RICHARD. No. You think something so untrue, all these years. I wasn't meeting anyone; it really was just an accident. I was worried about work. Some investments the firm had made, this huge account, something had gone wrong and someone was blaming it on me, it was all—I got this phone call. On our way out the door.

HELEN. A phone call?

RICHARD. You remember, the phone call.

HELEN. No, I don't remember a phone call—

RICHARD. And Lea—had already run, up ahead of me, but the call came in, I went back. Just for a minute. I thought she was just ahead of me. How many times did we take that path. Where you let them run, just ahead, around the next tree, you let them just get out of sight for a second, it wasn't like anything we hadn't done before. And then she wasn't there.

HELEN. It was more than a minute, Richard. She was gone. You didn't even know—how long, she was, at least as long as—you didn't even know, she was gone—

RICHARD. Helen—

HELEN. It was—

RICHARD. Don't go back there, please. This is meant to help you—

HELEN. Help me? How can you—it was five minutes, at least—

RICHARD. Listen to me. Helen. Listen. I'm trying to tell you, the truth. I didn't betray you. There was no other woman. You were what I wanted. You were always what I wanted.

(She looks at him, taking this in, confused, then looks away.)

HELEN. There's always that trick of time. When every moment feels right next to each other. When you remember exactly how you felt at the moment something happened years ago, I don't mean just this, so many moments, the moment we met, the moment I said I'd marry you, this moment, they stand so close, as if they were neighbors, as if there weren't twenty years between them. You think time is a train, that you go from place to place over long distances, but it's not, is it? It's all the same moment. And that movement, that sense of movement is some kind of fabrication, an optical illusion, maybe, life itself is an optical illusion. Is that possible?

    RICHARD. I don't know.

    HELEN. Your face. The familiarity of it, and the change. Yourself, but with time, only I don't know what time is. If I could just drown in your return. If I could drown in the present. Maybe all the rest would make sense. Maybe the all the moments could just be this moment.

(She looks at him. After a moment, she goes to him, and kisses him. The door to the house swings open, NATE appears.)

    NATE. Mom?

(He sees them kissing and stops, startled. HELEN takes a step backwards, and turns. They stare at each other.)

    HELEN. Yes?

    NATE. Oh I'm sorry, I, I—the last of the dishes are still, so I thought—to bring the rest, in inside so we could—

    HELEN. It's all right, Nate. We can get them in the morning.

    NATE. I can get them.

    HELEN. You should go to bed. Where's Erica?

    NATE. She's watching T.V., in her room.

    HELEN. You don't need to worry about the rest of the dishes. I'll take care of it, all right?

(He doesn't answer.)

    HELEN. *(Continuing)* It's fine, Nate. You go to bed.

(NATE stands in the doorway, for a moment. He goes, shutting the door behind him. HELEN kisses RICHARD again. Then, suddenly he takes her hand and goes to the bathtub, and turns on the water.)

RICHARD. What if they come out?
HELEN. I don't care if they do.

(He kisses her. She helps him to undress and get in, then goes to the table.)

HELEN. *(Continuing)* Do you want a drink?
RICHARD. Yeah.

(She pours him a drink.)

RICHARD. *(Continuing)* The air is so good here. The trees. The wind. *(Beat)* Are you coming?
HELEN. Yes.

(She turns and looks at RICHARD, who lies in the rising water, his eyes closed. She crosses, bringing him the drink. Blackout.)

Scene 5

(The following morning. The air is bright. There is a large tarp covering the tub. The dinner table, now cleared of all dishes, remains in place. LUCY is there, alone. She looks around, confused. NATE comes out. He stops, when he sees her.)

NATE. You're here.

LUCY. I got back last night, after midnight. Everyone seemed to be asleep. But the door was open, so I just — came in. And — went to bed.

(NATE starts to collapse the table and put it away.)

LUCY. *(Continuing.)* Have you seen Richard?

NATE. Oh, I, he left.

LUCY. Oh. Well, do you, do you know when he's coming back?

NATE. No, I don't know.

LUCY. Is he down at the lake?

NATE. I don't, I don't think so.

LUCY. He didn't sleep in our room last night.

NATE. *(Beat.)* Oh.

LUCY. And his stuff is gone. I mean, it's not in my room anymore, so I guess that's just, well, no surprise, huh. Anyway. I just wanted to tell him I'm going home, I don't know why I even bother, it seems polite. To say good-bye. Don't you think? Whatever. Did he say where he was going? *(NATE continues to move the table, and the chairs.)*

NATE. No. I I I don't know where Richard is. I maybe, may may — maybe Mom — I — I don't —

LUCY. It's OK, Nate. Serves me right, I should have known better than to get involved with any guy that fast, especially an older guy.

NATE. You couldn't know. What was going to happen. You just couldn't know.

LUCY. *(A beat.)* They're back together, aren't they?

NATE. *(Looks away.)* I don't know.

LUCY. I don't care. I mean, I just feel stupid. When things go like that, everything just gets so messy and hideous when it's not necessary! To drag me all the way up here, so he could get back together with his ex-wife? I mean, that's twisted, right? That's twisted!

NATE. Yes!

LUCY. I shouldn't have left last night. You kept telling me not to go, and I knew — I mean I knew, at that point, what the score was. And why hang around, right? That's what I thought, I don't need to hang around for this! But I still — I just —

NATE. I know.

LUCY. I know you do, I know.

(The back door opens, and HELEN comes out.)

HELEN. Lucy. Good morning!

LUCY. Good morning. Um — do you know where Richard is?

HELEN. Has Nate told you about what happened last night?

LUCY. No, we just, I was looking for Richard.

HELEN. Oh, you didn't tell her? He left.

NATE. I told her.

LUCY. No, I mean, yes, he did say that. I just wondered if you knew when he'd be back. I would like to say good-bye to him.

HELEN. I'm sorry. You misunderstand me. He actually left. He decided this, coming here, was just too upsetting for everyone, at least for now. So he left.

LUCY. He left? You mean — left? Without his car?

HELEN. He caught a train back to Philadelphia. I assumed

he tried to get hold of you, didn't he call?

LUCY. No.

HELEN. Maybe he tried and couldn't get through. The cell phones are awful up here. Anyway, I think he assumed you would need the car to drive back. I think that's fine, Nate. It is dirt, after all.

(NATE nods, and sets down the broom.)

LUCY. So —

HELEN. This has been, as you know, so complicated and difficult for all of us. Just overwhelming. So when he decided to go, so suddenly, I frankly understood it. I think he wanted to give everyone a little room. Including himself.

LUCY. So, he — he left.

HELEN. Yes.

LUCY. When Nate said he left, I just, I didn't understand that. OK. Well, um, can I, can I use your phone?

HELEN. Of course.

(HELEN steps aside, as LUCY goes into the house. NATE watches, then looks at HELEN.)

NATE. It's cold this morning.

HELEN. It is a little brisk. Here, let me warm you up.

(She goes and hugs him. He pushes her away. She looks at him. ERICA comes out, still in pajamas, carrying a cup of coffee and a piece of toast.)

ERICA. Hey.

HELEN. Good morning.

ERICA. Is something going on?

HELEN. What do you mean?

ERICA. Well, that Lucy person's in the kitchen, she looks kind of bent out of shape.

(LUCY comes out, carrying a phone.)

LUCY. He's not answering his phone.

HELEN. Perhaps he turned it off.

LUCY. Well, what time did he leave?

HELEN. Eleven, eleven-thirty?

ERICA. Dad left? Where'd he go?

HELEN. I don't know.

ERICA. He left? Without saying good-bye?

HELEN. Back to Philadelphia, at least that's what he said.

ERICA. He left? Without saying good-bye?

HELEN. He didn't want to wake you up.

ERICA. *(Sudden.)* Oh, fuck him. Fucking asshole. *(She goes into the house.)*

LUCY. He left without saying good-bye?

HELEN. He said good-bye to Nate.

LUCY. He did?

(She turns to NATE. There is a beat.)

NATE. Yes.

LUCY. Oh. 'Cause you didn't — I'm sorry. I'm just confused. Because before, you didn't —

NATE. *(Looking away.)* Mom took him to the train station.

LUCY. OK. Sure.

HELEN. I know, it's disorienting.

LUCY. It is, a bit.

HELEN. I told him — well what does it matter what I told him, he never did what I asked anyway. Is there anything I can do for you? Before you go?

LUCY. No, I'm sorry. This has just been — *(Beat.)* I'll go get my stuff.

(She goes into the house, sudden. HELEN looks at NATE.)

HELEN. It's all right, sweetheart.

(NATE starts to cry. She goes to him. He pushes her away.)

NATE. Don't, don't.

HELEN. I know. It's so upsetting. Him coming at all has been hard on all of us. But listen to me, Nate. It's going to be alright again. It's going to be just like it was.

NATE. Is it?

HELEN. Yes, it is. Everything is fine.

(LUCY enters, more upset, with the phone. ERICA enters behind her, curious now.)

LUCY. You know, I just checked my messages and he didn't call.

HELEN. Didn't he?

LUCY. No he didn't, and I hope you don't think I'm nuts — but this just doesn't make sense.

ERICA. Nothing makes sense. Welcome to our lives. When you see Richard, please tell him to go fuck himself.

HELEN. Erica.

ERICA. No. It's fine. Who needs him. But I'll tell you, if he comes back and tries to take the house again, we are going to hammer him in court. Hammer him.

LUCY. What train did he take? I'm calling the station.

(She starts to dial. HELEN crosses, quick, and takes the phone from her in an abrupt gesture. LUCY looks at her.)

HELEN. Look. You're working yourself up, over nothing. Everybody knows this was an extraordinary situation. Richard felt that he had pushed it as far as he could, and he needed to go. I'm sorry if you can't understand that. Other than that, I don't know what to say to you. I don't know you, and I don't care what you think.

ERICA. OK? Is that good enough for you?

LUCY. No, it's not.

ERICA. You've been dumped. You'll survive.

LUCY. This isn't about being dumped!

ERICA. I'm sure.

NATE. Leave her alone! She's not stupid, she's just — leave her alone!

(There is a momentary silence at this.)

ERICA. *(A dawning doubt.)* What are you so bent out of shape about?

NATE. Nothing happened! It's what Mom said! He's just gone! That's all, he's gone! I mean, just stop it! Everybody, just,

God, this is, all of you — I can't, this is, please! It's done, you can't make it go back! It's, all of it is done. *(Beat.)* My head is all white.

(*HELEN looks at LUCY, then goes to NATE.*)

HELEN. Come on, sweetheart, let me take you inside.

NATE. *(Yelling at her.)* Stay away from me! *(Beat.)* I'm sorry. I'm sorry. But God, you just can't touch me now, don't you see that?

ERICA. Mom?

HELEN. He's fine, Erica.

ERICA. What — what —

NATE. I didn't do it. You know that. I wouldn't. I just helped, after. It was too late, it was just too late. What else could I do? It wasn't her fault.

ERICA. *(Harsh.)* What wasn't?

HELEN. Erica, I think you should take your brother inside.

NATE. She knows, anyway! It wouldn't matter, Mom, she would know any¬way.

(*There is a terrible pause at this.*)

ERICA. Know what? *(Quiet.)* Where is he?

NATE. *(Simple.)* What was I supposed to do? Mom? You were asleep. You fall asleep with the TV on. But someone had to help her, after. What else was I supposed to do? It was too late anyway. It was just too late.

ERICA. *(A beat.)* You helped her what?

NATE. It was too late!

(ERICA sits, silent. There is a moment of silence.)

ERICA. Mom?

(NATE pulls the tarp off the bathtub; it is drenched in blood.)

HELEN. It didn't have to happen, Erica. I mean, it's not like I went looking for him. And believe me, he knew it would be a mistake to come back. But he couldn't let it go. You don't understand, you're too young, and frankly, I've tried to protect you from all of this. So many things you didn't know. My silence, everything you blame me for, that was protection, so no, you can't understand. He said, last night, that he wanted to step back into the center of his nature. That meant, all of it. All of us. Forgiving him, moving on. He wanted everything, so many men do. They want their crime and their forgiveness too, more than forgiveness, they want the earth itself to rise up and erase the worst of everything they do, no responsibility, action without consequence, everything is still theirs, that's what they want! And I'm not going to lie to you. Most of them get it. And it's a sin. The erasure of justice? We can't survive it. As a people. It has deformed us, this insistence that men, with their power and their selfishness and their cruelty can crawl the Earth and destroy everything, everything, and no one holds them to account. Justice? Do you know what kind of justice I was offered when he murdered my child? The police came, then, and ruled it an accident. To be told endlessly it was no one's fault. Last night I heard it all again, he wasn't responsible, he simply went into his head and that's why it happened. Because he was absorbed

in the intricacies of his endlessly fascinating mind, his child disappeared in the wood, and then into the water, she disappeared
from this Earth and he was not responsible. How could he help
going into his head and worrying about nothing? It wasn't even
nothing, to him, even now, it was still important to him, these
things in his head, he was telling me, there was someone, at his
work, looking to blame him for some loss of revenue, do these
words mean anything? To anyone? *(Laughing.)* To him, they
still did. He had justification. It wasn't his fault. He offered this
to me — seriously — as something that might heal me! He was
all concerned, at one time, in my rage I accused him of betray-
ing me, I was hungry, for some absurd meaning, if he had fallen
in love, perhaps, his passion led him and all of us astray, that
was something, I thought, for a moment, years ago, that might
have been a reality, something to explain the inexplicable, how
can you let your child drown, before your eyes? How can you
do it? And he took that lame hope from me, as a gift, no, there
was no other woman! If there was any blame, it was mine. We
should have gone through it together. I was somehow not wom-
anly enough, the failure was mine, I should have risen from the
tragedy like an angel and wiped his crime away from his brow.
Like a mother. Well, I am a mother. Over time, all this time, that
is what I have been, and there has been too much time given to
me. You don't know how hard I prayed, year in and year out,
for the rage and the bitterness to leave me, for it to grow into
some larger meaning, I begged whatever is out there to reveal
to me how to move on, I lived with nature, I cared for the children who were left to me as if they were life itself, I held them
to me as protection against all of it and still there was nothing!
You pray for justice and the gods laugh. You pray for peace and
they abandon you. A moments peace. He had it. That is what he

brought here, to me. The sight of his peace. The yearning to be together. Again. To move forward. To leave it behind. Well, I gave him what he wanted. We finished it, together, the only way it could be finished. And I have no remorse. *(Then, to LUCY.)* Call the police. I don't care. I have my peace now, and God knows I've earned it. *(She goes into the house.)*

ERICA. Nate? You helped her?

NATE. Yeah. I did. She came up to my room and she was covered in — and I went down, and he, he was —

ERICA. Oh my God.

NATE. We had to. Because Lea. You remember. How wild she was? She would like throw herself off the furniture, you had to follow her, she was always throwing herself into into the lake.

ERICA. What are you talking about?

NATE. *(Overlap.)* You and me, you didn't have to watch you and me! The lake scared me to, and you were born knowing how to swim but Lea — and he just let her run down the path! Like it was oh, we did it all the time, but only a fucking moron would let that kid run down to the lake, she was the one you didn't take your eyes off! And he, ten minutes, at least —

ERICA. Did Mom tell you this? That makes it OK to kill him? Is that what she said?

NATE. It's just true. Fuck it. We have to finish cleaning it up, now.

LUCY. We have to call the police.

ERICA. I'll do it. Nate don't. Don't touch anything. Don't clean anything.

LUCY. We have to do it now, Erica, right now!

ERICA. *(Overlap.)* I'm doing it! *(To NATE.)* If you try to cover it up it'll just be worse. This can't get any worse. But the

cops will just think it's worse, everybody will think it's worse.
So just don't, just don't clean anymore, OK?

NATE. You're going to call the cops?

ERICA. Of course we're calling the cops!

NATE. What are you going to tell them?

ERICA. I'm gonna tell them — you have to tell them what,
happened —

NATE. I'm not talking to them. I'm not talking to anybody.
I have to clean this.

(NATE pushes by them and goes to the hose.)

ERICA. I don't think that's a good idea!

LUCY. Just dial the phone, Erica, what are you waiting
for?

ERICA. Would you give me a minute?

LUCY. We don't have a minute, this is murder!

ERICA. I'm aware of that! THERE'S BLOOD ALL OVER
MY BACKYARD. This sucks. This is a nightmare.

NATE. You didn't even have to do it! You didn't have to do
anything! I don't know what you're complaining about!

ERICA. What am I COMPLAINING ABOUT? Nate, I
know you're only half with us most of the time, but I mean,
you're kidding, right? You are just fucking KIDDING ME.

NATE. I'm not. You didn't have to do it. I mean, you might
think about that.

ERICA. I DON'T WANT TO THINK.

NATE. Yeah, me neither, but then what you're left with? Is
what you do. You can sit there, go ahead and sit there, you never
had to do anything —

ERICA. Don't you fucking defend yourself —

NATE. *(Overlap.)* He was here. Naked. Covered in — and I did it. She said, and I just, I went down to the basement and got the garbage bags, and the twine, and the bricks —

ERICA. *(Overlap.)* Stop it, I don't want to know!

NATE. *(Overlap.)* His blood. Everywhere. My own — father — and I — drenched. Drenched! I had to pick him up, she couldn't even so I dragged him. To his own boat. And we, out there, on the lake. I did it. You didn't.

ERICA. What's your point, Nate? Are you fucking proud of yourself?

NATE. I'm just saying what happened. What I did, that you didn't. It makes us different now.

LUCY. Nate. It wasn't your fault.

NATE. *(Furious at her.)* I know it wasn't my fault! It happened because it had to happen! Because she — . And I did it. Because I'm such a good boy, I'm such a, whatever she said, I just, if she told me to chop him into little pieces, cook him up and have him for dinner, I would have done it! Why? Because I love her? No! He deserved it! They both deserve it! That's the next thing, isn't it?

LUCY. What?

NATE. I don't want to hurt anybody. But that's what, that's what —

LUCY. No no no —

NATE. Isn't it? Erica?

ERICA. You're crazy.

NATE. Am I?

LUCY. No, come on —

(NATE is focused on ERICA, watching her figure it out.)

NATE. She showed me how to do it.

LUCY. *(Overlap.)* Nate. You don't want to hurt anybody.

NATE. She said, you have to help me. And the thing is, it's horrible, and there's so much, but once you say, I'm doing this, it's just something you're doing.

LUCY. *(Overlap.)* No no, it's not, you're not —

NATE. *(Overlap.)* It's not as hard as you think.

LUCY. *(Overlap.)* Listen to me, please, both of you —

NATE. *(Overlap.)* She's the same. She's just as bad, she's worse! She's like one of those animals who eats her young.

LUCY. Nate.

NATE. Shut up! That's the way it is, in nature. There isn't any justice. There's just the thing that comes next.

LUCY. Nobody thinks —

NATE. I said, shut the fuck up!

ERICA. I'm calling the police.

NATE. *(Grabs the phone from her.)* Why? This doesn't have anything to do with them. It doesn't mean anything if they do it. It's just television then. They think they know things out there, they don't know anything. There's no justice, not even in their world. Is that what you want? A trial? Because I don't want that. I want this. It may not mean anything? But it's true. Don't you? Want to?

LUCY. Nate, come on. You don't know what you're saying now, we can we —

(She grabs his arm, to talk to him. He shoves her aside and turns back to ERICA.)

NATE. Both of them. It was always about, who was going to win. They took our lives from us! To satisfy their own, all of it, they were supposed to, our parents! And neither one of us ever even existed. Well, I exist now. It has to be both of them.

ERICA. No. No! I didn't want him to come back, it was too hard, but he — he wanted me. He came back. For me. She never, it was always you —

NATE. No —

ERICA. And now I don't have anyone. Fuck this! Just fuck it.

(She starts to go away from him. He suddenly grabs her.)

NATE. You have me.

ERICA. I know.

NATE. I love you more than anybody. More than her. I do.

ERICA. I know, Nate.

NATE. She was the one who took him from you.

ERICA. I know.

NATE. *(Quiet.)* I would do it, for you.

LUCY. Nate, stop it. Both of you. It doesn't have to keep going!

NATE. If it doesn't have to, then why does it?

LUCY. No no, listen to me —

NATE. We could do it. Together. We could finish it. It would be over.

LUCY. Listen — we can go. Now, right now, before something . . .

NATE. *(Laughing.)* Before something happens?

LUCY. Nate. Come on. Please. You don't have to do anything that you don't, in your heart you —

(He turns, furious, hits her in the stomach, hard. She hits the ground. He cocks his arm, about to strike her again.)

ERICA. Chill out, Nate. *(Then, to LUCY.)* You know, people been telling you for days that you don't belong here. What exactly is it gonna take for you to get the message?

(LUCY scrambles to her feet, then turns, and suddenly goes.)

NATE. Is she gone?
ERICA. Yeah.
NATE. Good.

(He looks out at the trees.)

NATE. *(Continuing.)* You know all those books?
ERICA. What books?
NATE. All those books people write. And then other people read.
ERICA. Oh, those books.
NATE. They're all full of shit. I mean, look at the trees!
ERICA. What about them?
NATE. They're red.

(HELEN stands in the doorway. She steps out.)

HELEN. Is that person gone?
NATE. Yes. She's gone.
HELEN. Thank God. Now maybe we can have a little peace. Nate?

(She looks at the bathtub.)

NATE. I'll finish it, Mom.

HELEN. Thank you, sweetheart. You're such a good boy. Oh, I feel so much better! Your father suggested last night he should have made me leave long ago and I had to completely resist the urge to laugh in his face. I just mean. How could you leave a place like this? The earth is so beautiful here. How could you ever leave?

(She looks up at the trees, happy. NATE and ERICA sit beside her on the steps of the porch.)

(The lights fade.)

END OF PLAY

MAURITIUS
Theresa Rebeck

Comedy / 3m, 2f / Interior

Stamp collecting is far more risky than you think. After their mother's death, two estranged half-sisters discover a book of rare stamps that may include the crown jewel for collectors. One sister tries to collect on the windfall, while the other resists for sentimental reasons. In this gripping tale, a seemingly simple sale becomes dangerous when three seedy, high-stakes collectors enter the sisters' world, willing to do anything to claim the rare find as their own.

"(Theresa Rebeck's) belated Broadway bow, the only original play by a woman to have its debut on Broadway this fall."
- Robert Simonson, *New York Times*

"*Mauritius* caters efficiently to a hunger that Broadway hasn't been gratifying in recent years. That's the corkscrew-twist drama of suspense… she has strewn her script with a multitude of mysteries."
- Ben Brantley, *New York Times*

"Theresa Rebeck is a slick playwright… Her scenes have a crisp shape, her dialogue pops, her characters swagger through an array of showy emotion, and she knows how to give a plot a cunning twist."
- John Lahr, *The New Yorker*